lonely planet KIDS

Happiness
Around the World

A Global Guide to Joyfulness

WORDS BY KATE BAKER

PICTURES BY WAZZA PINK

Acknowledgements

Author: Kate Baker
Illustrator: Wazza Pink
Publisher: Piers Pickard
Art Director: Andy Mansfield
Editorial Director: Joe Fullman
Commissioning Editor: Kate Baker
Print Production: Nigel Longuet

Published in October 2022 by Lonely Planet Global Ltd

CRN: 554153 • ISBN: 978 1 83869 510 1
www.lonelyplanet.com/kids • © Lonely Planet 2022

Printed in China
2 4 6 8 10 9 7 5 3 1

Stay in touch – lonelyplanet.com/contact

Ireland
Digital Depot, Roe Lane (off Thomas St),
Digital Hub, Dublin 8, D08 TCV4

To Freddie,
who showed me the true meaning of happiness.
—K.B.

To my dear life companion and my dear friends,
I don't need to find joy in anywhere faraway thanks to you.
—W.P.

Happiness is a feeling you just can't hide,
a warm fuzzy glow that grows inside.

Come travel around the world and see
what happiness means to you and me...

In Brazil,
happiness is joining the Carnival parade.

Every year, the Brazilian city of Rio de Janeiro hosts one of the biggest parties in the world - Carnival!

Millions of people take part. They wear colourful costumes and parade through the streets alongside floats - decorated platforms on wheels. Some outfits are covered in beautiful feathers, like tropical birds. There is lots of dancing, and people make music by drumming, jangling bells, tooting horns and blowing whistles. Visitors from all over the globe come to join in the festival fun!

In Mexico,
happiness is remembering dead ancestors.

The Day of the Dead festival takes place every November throughout Mexico.

People hold parties, paint their faces like skeletons and leave presents on homemade altars to welcome their lost loved ones back into the world of the living. Candles are lit so the spirits can find their way home, and food is laid out in case they are hungry after their long journey. Instead of being a sad day, it is a joyful time to think about family members who have passed away and to celebrate their lives.

In the USA,
happiness is a meal with family.

Whether it's Thanksgiving or someone's birthday, nothing says happiness like a family feast.

People in the USA love getting together for a big meal. This can take place at any time of year. In autumn and winter, family feasts usually take place inside with everyone gathered around a large table. In summer, people might have their food outside at a cook-out or barbecue. These are times to be with those you love, and to think of all the things you are grateful for – such as the food on your table, friendships and family.

In Denmark, happiness is being cosy.

Hygge (pronounced 'hoo-ga') is a
Danish word meaning 'cosiness'.

*H*ygge is putting on some warm woolly socks and snuggling on the sofa on a cold night. It is listening to the crackle of a roaring fire or being inside reading a book on a rainy day. It is mugs of hot chocolate, sweet buns and the warm glow of candlelight. It is also family get-togethers, picnics in the park, friendship and laughter – all the cosy everyday moments that make you smile.

In Italy,
happiness is an evening stroll.

As the sun goes down, Italians of all ages put on their smart clothes and go for a *passeggiata* – a slow walk through the town.

Along the way, they stop to chat and laugh with friends, while enjoying the last rays of sunlight. Walking with family or friends can cheer you up, and fresh air and exercise are good for you too!

Caffè

In Finland, happiness is having a sauna.

A sauna is a small heated room made steamy by pouring water onto hot rocks.

Sauna bathing has been a family tradition in Finland for hundreds of years. The heat makes you feel calm and peaceful, and it is also thought to keep you healthy. After getting hot and sweaty, you can go outside and dive into an ice-cold lake or roll in fresh powdery snow. Some say that every sauna is looked after by a *saunatonttu* (sauna elf) who bathes in the steam after the people have gone!

In Mali,
happiness is dancing to the beat of drums.

The *djembe* drum was supposedly first played for the King of Mali hundreds of years ago.

It was played from mountaintop to mountaintop to let people know that the king was coming and to bring everyone together in celebration. Today, people still sing and dance to the sound of the *djembe* to celebrate all kinds of important life events, such as the birth of a child or getting married, to tell stories, or just to feel good!

In India,
happiness is yoga.

Thousands of years ago, the ancient yogis (people who practise yoga) lived in the forests and mountains of India.

They looked at the nature around them – animals and plants, rivers and mountains, the sun and stars – and copied their movements. Yoga isn't just about stretching your body. Breathing slowly and clearing your mind of busy thoughts helps you to feel calm and content. Say hello to the sun, stand tall like a tree and feel your worries drift away!

In China,
happiness is tidying up.

The Chinese New Year festival has been celebrated for thousands of years.

To prepare for the festival, people must first clean and tidy their homes. Windows are washed, floors are swept and every corner is dusted. It is thought that doing this will clear away the bad luck of the past year and bring good luck and happiness for the new year ahead. Many people believe that keeping your home clean and clear of clutter can make you feel happier and more relaxed. So, get your duster ready and start tidying!

In South Korea, happiness is singing.

Going to a *noraebang* (singing room) is one of the most popular ways of having fun with friends in South Korea.

Inside, there are shiny disco lights, video screens showing the words to the songs, and microphones for you to sing into. Scientists say that singing releases special chemicals in your brain that make you feel good. It doesn't matter if you can't sing in tune, so long as you have a good time. Sing loud and clear for all to hear!

In Japan,
happiness is bathing in a forest.

Shinrin–yoku is a Japanese tradition that means to 'forest bathe'.

If you ever feel sad, go for a walk in a forest or spend some time in nature and your spirits will soon lift! Walk slowly and enjoy the sights, sounds and smells. Watch how the sunlight falls on the leaves, listen to the birdsong and the wind rushing through the trees. Explore under rocks and logs, and breathe in the fresh clean air. This is forest bathing!

In Tokelau,
happiness is sharing.

On the Pacific islands of Tokelau, villagers take part in a *faiva fakamua* (fishing quest).

Early in the evening, the men and boys of the islands set out in search of fish to feed their whole village. The next morning, the fresh catch is laid out on the beach, then shared among all the villagers. The fishermen are greeted by the girls and women serving cups of tea. It is easy to share. It makes others feel good and makes you feel good too!

In Australia,
happiness is telling stories.

From an early age, Aboriginal children listen to
tales that explain the world around them.

The stories are told by the elders and passed down from generation to generation. Sitting by a campfire as night falls, they recall stories about how the stars got in the sky. They tell tales about their ancestors, the land and the animals and how they came to be. These stories help the children learn about their culture and how to live in harmony with the people and animals around them.

Dance to the beat, sing as loud as you can,
give thanks, take a stroll, lend someone a hand.

There are so many things that you can do,
for happiness is something that lives in you.

What makes YOU happy?